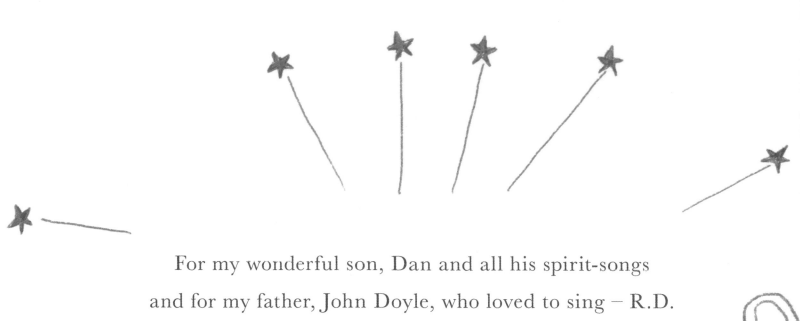

For my wonderful son, Dan and all his spirit-songs
and for my father, John Doyle, who loved to sing – R.D.

For Mae Doyle – A.L.

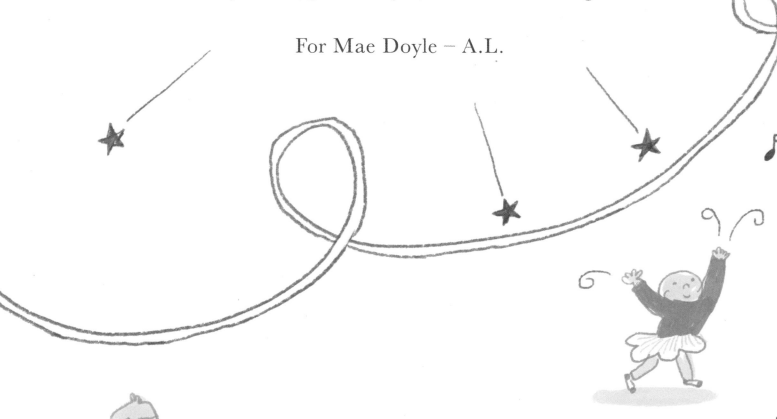

First published in Great Britain in 2020 by Andersen Press Ltd.,

20 Vauxhall Bridge Road, London SW1V 2SA.

Text copyright © Ruth Doyle 2020.

Illustration copyright © Ashling Lindsay 2020.

The rights of Ruth Doyle and Ashling Lindsay to be identified

as the author and illustrator of this work have been asserted by them in

accordance with the Copyright, Designs and Patents Act, 1988.

All rights reserved. Printed and bound in Italy.

3   5   7   9   10   8   6   4   2

British Library Cataloguing in Publication Data available.

ISBN 978 1 78344 850 0

Songs
for our
Sons

RUTH DOYLE

ASHLING LINDSAY

Andersen Press

Born on this
star-scattered night,
kissed by the cosmos –
A child made of
moonbeams.

In your newborn cry,
songs of peace
long for release.
So unfurl your fragile
fists, little one.

The world holds its breath at
the wonders you bring
All coiled-up potential,
like a seedling in spring.

So dance-up your dreams;
sing out your spirit-song
And let the light that's inside you,
guide you along.

Never change,
fib or follow,
just to try to fit in.
Be proud, free and happy in
your own, unique skin.

Be a sequinned sparkler,
a dynamic dazzler,
a kaleidoscopic
colour-catcher.

Or a rain-bouncing,
puddle-pouncing,
soil-squelching
mud sculptor!

Honour your huge heart –
your feelings are real
And pain is a big deal
that crying can heal.

If anger
invades you,

breathe out

long and slow

And let in the joy,

as the bad

feelings go.

Your true power and value
can't be measured by size

So don't judge or be judged by
what's seen with the eyes.

Be a
nature-explorer,
a wonder-discoverer
See the shapes inside
snowflakes, the path
that the hare takes,

Hear the rhythms the rain makes;
birds singing as day breaks.

Keep a still place inside,

that you can call home

And know how to find it,

wherever you roam.

Weave wise words as weapons,
be a barrier-breaking rapper

A champion of change,
a fearless truth-writer

A tender defender and
non-violent fighter.

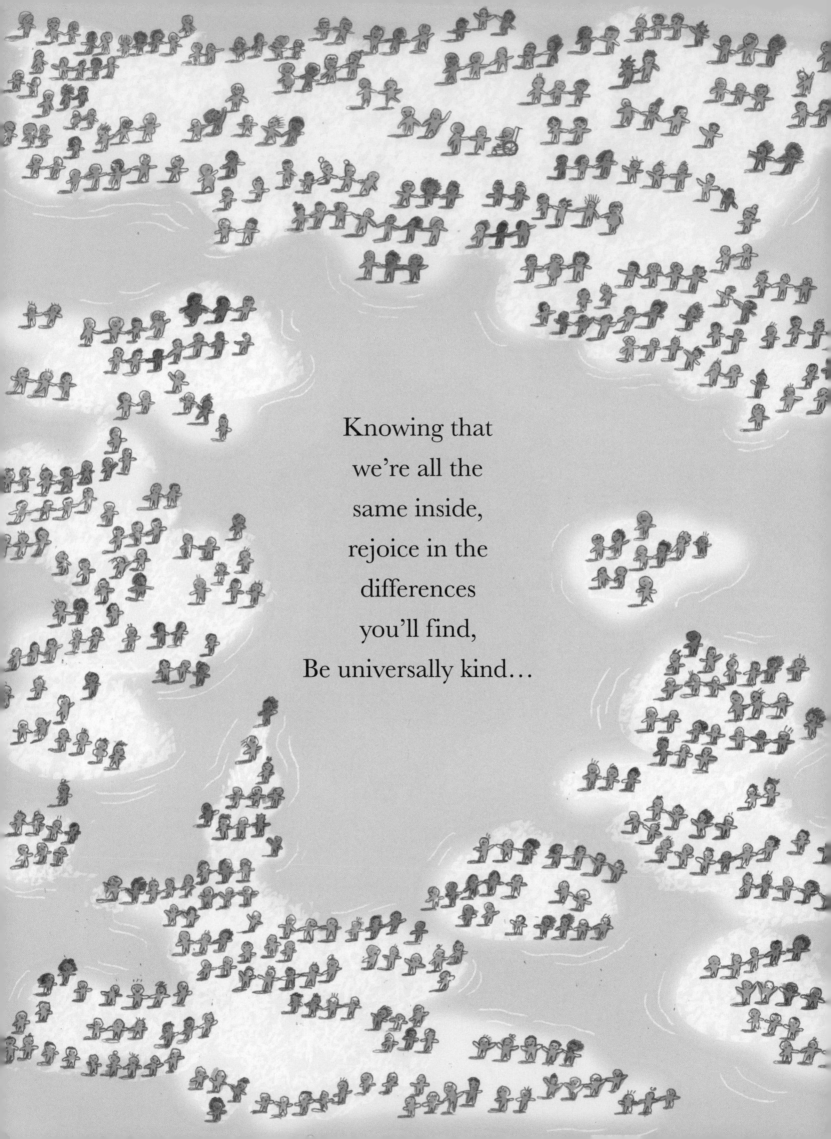

Knowing that
we're all the
same inside,
rejoice in the
differences
you'll find,
Be universally kind…

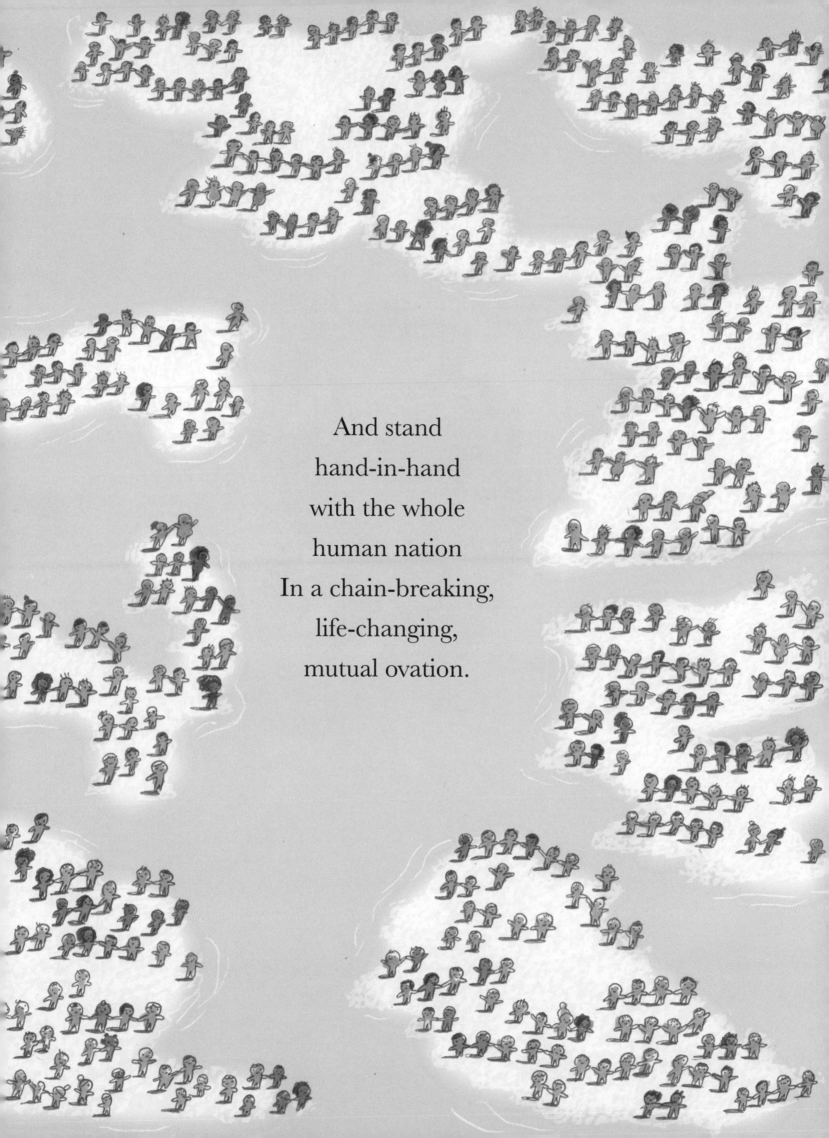

And stand
hand-in-hand
with the whole
human nation
In a chain-breaking,
life-changing,
mutual ovation.

So get ready for life,
planet earth has been waiting
For the gift that is you
and the hope you're creating.

Sing the song of your heart,
be an enlightened wrong-righter
And help build a world
so much gentler and brighter.